An Alcoholic's Story

An Alcoholic's Story

William Tedesco

Order this book online at www.trafford.com
or email orders@trafford.com

Most Trafford titles are also available at major online book retailers.

Printed in Victoria, BC, Canada.

ISBN: 978-1-4269-2967-0

*Our mission is to efficiently provide the world's finest, most comprehensive
book publishing service, enabling every author to experience success.
To find out how to publish your book, your way, and have it available
worldwide, visit us online at www.trafford.com*

Trafford rev. 4/27/2010

 www.trafford.com

North America & international
toll-free: 1 888 232 4444 (USA & Canada)
phone: 250 383 6864 ✦ fax: 812 355 4082

I'm going to tell you a story of alcoholism that traveled through a family. It's a story of the abuse that the children of alcoholics live with and how it tears a family apart. About relatives that I feel were alcoholics, even though I can't take everybody's inventory. How parents spread alcoholism to their kids and how their kids became parents and spread it on. It is a family disease, and it can travel from generation to generation. I hope you read it and it helps you.

Thank you.

An Alcoholic's Story

My father was born in another country as an American citizen. When my grandmother was expecting my dad, she went to Italy to visit her farm, which was being taken care of by others.

When my grandmother was born, she was promised to somebody for marriage. That man would later become my grandfather. They were cousins, which was common back then. When my grandmother turned sixteen, they were married. My grandfather lived in Pittsburgh, Pennsylvania. At the time, my grandfather was a heavy drinker and beat my grandmother a lot. Grandma and Grandpa had six kids, with my father being the baby of the family.

I guess my father witnessed this abuse and thought it was normal.

My dad came back to the United States in 1934 when he was three years old. He was put in a Catholic home because there was a depression at the time, and Grandpa had died from alcoholism. My dad spent the next seven years in the home, until he was ten years old.

Grandma signed the wrong papers and lost everything—her money, her apartment building, and her shoe repair business. They were broke. My grandma liked to drink wine every day. My dad got caught stealing a dress and spent another two years in another home for Grandma. His sister, my Aunt Gloria, was there also.

My father respected his mother to the utmost and did whatever she said. He used to sell bags on the corners of N.Y. He was able to buy them for a half of a penny and sell them for a penny to help feed his family. In the sixth grade he quit school.

When he was a little kid, my father was beat up a lot by a black kid. Because my Aunt Gloria was older, she made him fight that black kid who had beat him up. When my father grew older, he boxed in the Golden Gloves. He was good, and the Italians wanted him to fight professionally, but my grandma said no way, even though he enjoyed beating the hell out somebody. My father hated the blacks and said they were nothing but niggers and that everybody should own them.

By this time, my dad's sisters in 1943 were getting married. My Aunt Nelda was left in Italy taking care of her grandparent during World War II, and some of them went their separate ways. The rest of the family moved to Muskegon, Michigan. My dad joined the Navy, but he was forced to leave when they found out he was only sixteen.

My dad met a girl named Gloria and fell in love with her. Their first son was born when he was only seventeen. Gloria's family was Mexican, and they forbade her to married him. Out of anger, my dad joined the Army but was dishonorably discharged for knocking out his commanding officer. His platoon went to Korea, and everybody was killed except him. I guess God was on his side.

He had a friend named Charlie who was also Italian. They met in Muskegon. Charlie introduced him to my mother, and they started to date. My mom was a sweet person—nice and meek—and wasn't use to being with somebody raised in New York City. My dad weighed 140 pounds and could bench press about 225 pounds. He had some build, and he could fight anybody. He always believed that you should never let anybody touch you or take anything from you. One night he and my mom went to the movies, and a guy in the row in front of them hit my dad in the head with a bottle. My dad got up and beat the hell out of the man and a second man who was with him, which led to him being put out of the movies. It turned out that one of these two guys was named

Don, and he and my dad became the best of friends. At this point in time, my dad wasn't drinking heavily yet.

One night Mom and Dad went to his family's house for dinner. The Italians start with a salad first, and then they come out with the meatball and sausage. To start off the meal, Mom went and ate the whole salad by herself. Everyone at the table started laughing, and my grandma asked Dad in Italian if she ate at home. My father was a catch in his time. All girls wanted him, but my mom wasn't going to let anybody have him.

My mom told my grandma dad raped her. My dad denied it, but Grandma made him married my mother. ?? In 1950 Mom and Dad were married. They went to New York City, and by this time Mom liked her beer and started to drink. Dad was a drinker but only on holidays or a few on the weekends. Mom was homesick, so they came back to Muskegon. In June of 1951 my brother Roger was born. In an Italian home the first son is usually named after the father, but Mom was angry at him and named him Roger instead.

My dad was working in a body shop. When he was little, he was good with art, so he took his art and used it on the cars he worked on—he was fast and good. He had a little toolbox and the other bodymen laugh at him. He did twice the work as the other men in the shop in addition to doing piecework and made twice the money. As they did they laugh no more. My mom always said he made great money. He would buy cars, fix them, and sell them for extra money. We always had food on the table. Mom and Dad still fought, and Mom was still drinking more than Dad. Dad would have a beer or two with a hot dog or a sandwich. Mom usually had a beer or scotch.

My sister Virginia was born in December 1954 and was named after my grandmother. Dad's drinking was still the same. After Virginia was born, Dad started his own body shop. Everybody knew he was a good body man. He used to like painting the most. My parents' marriage was becoming rocky. In November 1957 I was born, and Mom named me after my father. All the kids had dark hair and dark eyes, but I came out with blonde hair and hazel eyes. Right away, my dad assumed I wasn't his, but my mom had blonde hair and hazel eyes. I took after my mother, but I looked like him. Dad wasn't the brightest at that time.

We never stayed in one place to long. Dad wanted to move to California. Aunt Virginia, Aunt Rita, and Aunt Gloria all live there. When I was born, I was a sick child. At ten months old, I almost died, but my dad saved my life. In California, when I was four to five years old, I almost died again. I was three when we moved to California. Dad's drinking took off, and he was drinking every night. Living in California was a big party to him. We moved from one place to another often, and Mom and Dad were both drinking more and more. Dad was fighting a lot and causing problems. One day my brother had a problem with two older men, and my father beat the hell out of one of them. He knocked one of the men out and broke his nose on top of it ask the other guy come on and the guy pick up his friend and took off. They quickly found out about Dad and how he could fight.

My dad's life revolved around alcohol, fighting, and strange women. I believe that if AIDS had existed back then, he would have contracted it. Mom became homesick again, so we packed up and went back to Muskegon. I was about seven years old. Dad opened another body shop and an Italian restaurant—life was good. He was making money hand over fist. Then, in April 1964, my mom had their last child. Joanna had brown hair and brown eyes, and I was screwed for sure. I was the only blonde child, so Dad started to hate me even more because I was the black sheep. I respected him and loved him so much, and he disliked me. I would try to satisfy him in every way, because I was proud to be his son.

Dad came home one day, and out of the blue, we were moving again. He had gotten in trouble with a woman in Michigan, so we move to Florida. When we were leaving, the police pulled us over. There was a warrant for his arrest. The police office told him if he would leave, he would close his eyes. Dad and the police didn't get along—his drinking and fighting caused him a lot of problems. Living in Florida was something—no more winters. The snow in Michigan is bad. He started to complain about the money he was making. He would take my sister and me roller skating every Saturday, and that was an excuse for him to go to the bars.

One time my older brother was working with Dad at the body shop. They left and went to a Cuban bar where Dad told everybody he hated Cubans. He beat the hell out of somebody, came out, and wanted to go to another bar and do it again. My brother thought he was crazy. One Christmas he bought me and my sister roller skates and then took them back to the store. He ruined our Christmas.

Mom received a hospital bill owing nine hundred dollars. Mom asked Dad who he had knocked up. Dad had another son. We then moved to New Jersey, and that's when my life went to hell. I still loved him and respected him, but now I was afraid of him. My childhood started to suck. Dad was working in a dealership, and we were living in a hotel. My Uncle Joe still lived in the Bronx, and Dad took us there for dinner. Mom always liked to through the bowery and China Town. In the bowery the winos washed your windows with water bottles and dried them with newspaper. Mom told me they were alcoholics. We would go to China Town, and a black guy would walk up to Dad and ask him if he wanted to buy a watch worth $250 for $25. Dad said he did the same thing when he was a kid in New York—fancy face, fancy back, and a piece of shit in the middle, Dad would laugh.

We went by my uncle's for dinner and got food poisoning. Everybody ate the Italian sausage except Dad and we ate soup for a week. Dad and Mom were talking about going back to Michigan when a salesman said he managed two apartment buildings in Passaic, New Jersey, and had an empty apartment. Dad had to get us back in school, so we moved to Passaic where we lived in the slums on the east side. After the move, I started running around with the bad kids. One friend in particular got me in trouble all the time—Ray. My dad hated Ray and gave me a beating every time he heard I was hanging out with him. One time when I was ten, Joe, Ray, and I went to Coney Island, and they left me there. The police took me back to the bus station and put me on a bus back to New Jersey. At the time, there were riots over Martin Luther King Jr.'s murder. The Passaic police called Dad, and he had to meet me at the bus in Garfield. He asked me what the hell was I doing in Coney Island and beat the hell out of me and forbid me to hang out with Ray.

When I was seven years old my friend's grandfather tried to molest me. When I told my father, he went nuts and came home drunk that night. I was so screwed up over that. When I was nine years old, I started to smoke; when I was ten, I started to sniff carbonia spot remover and glue. When I was eleven years old, I met a couple that I liked and would go over to their house to visit. One day when the man and I were alone, he tried to molest me. I ran out of the apartment and ran home. I told my mom, and she called Dad and then later called the police. Dad wanted to kill him, but the police got there first. Dad pulled up in a tow truck and wanted to beat him, chain him to the truck, and drag him all over Passaic. The police told Dad to calm down, and Dad told the man he was lucky and to thank God the police got there first.

On my twelfth birthday I started drinking with one of my brother's friends. I got drunk for the first time, and it made me forget about everything. I got home as my father was going out. He slapped me in the face and asked me where I was because Mom had bought me a birthday cake. I sobered up quickly, and he left and told mom I was drunk. Mom never said anything to Dad. One day later I fell asleep in Dad's bed (Mom and Dad weren't sleeping together anymore by this point). The man I looked up too and loved all these years tried to molest me. I was shock and didn't believe it. How could my dad do this to me? I told Mom, and she had him locked up. He ended up in the Passaic County Jail and called his friend Joe to bail him out. Joe came by before he bailed him out and asked what happen. Mom told him to ask me. Dad was fighting with other inmates in jail because they didn't like what he did, and Joe bailed him out. My life became a living hell. Because of what happen to me, the kids called me gay. My friend's older brothers were trying to molest me.

I was ashamed of what my father had done, so I started to drink to forget—I was only twelve years old. My mom was afraid of my father because he was Italian. He knew crazy people, and she figured he was in the mafia. What she didn't know was if the mafia found out what he did they would have to kill him. Dad came home all these years, and Mom knew he was sleeping with other women. She didn't know he was bisexual. Dad was drinking and drugging at this time.

Uncle Joe lived in New York in 1970 when he died of a heart attack caused by alcoholism. My dad and us went to the funeral. There were wine bottles everywhere. My father was very angry. My Aunt Virginia from California was there. My dad and I went for a walk. He was trying to be different toward me. He stopped for some Italian coffee and pastries. The Italians were talking to him in Italian telling him they were sorry to hear about Joe. Dad went to a card reader, and she told him there would be another death in the family within a year. Dad was upset, so he paid her and left. After the funeral, we returned home, and Aunt Virginia went back to California. Then Aunt Virginia had a bad accident in California, but they didn't expect her to live. Dad went nuts because he loved Virginia with all his heart. On June 20, 1971, Dad came home at two o'clock in the morning after a night of partying and said he would be dead by nine in the morning. Mom laughed, but at 8:45 am, my father died. We were in shock. I didn't know if

I should cry or be happy that we were finally out of his prison. My mom was a meek person. She loved us, but before my dad died, Ginger was seeing black guys. He beat her ass for that. Now he's gone so she started to see this black guy he was married. My older brother ran away and joined the Marine Corps.

My dad was also living when he did that. Joanna was only six years old when Dad died, so she didn't know anything about her father. I was thirteen years old, and I was ashamed of my life. I was kicked out of public school because I hit two black kids with a baseball bat. (My father was proud of that.) I continued to go to Catholic school after he died. I was drinking with my friends, which continued right into high school. I bottled up my childhood–all that did was cause me to drink more to forget. I didn't want to be me, so I tried to be somebody else. My life sucked. I didn't tell my new friends about my past.

I worked in high school. My brother got out of the Marine Corps, and my sister had a baby with a black man. My brother was a lot like our dad—he hated blacks. He wanted to kill Ginger. I worked in the print shop in high school, and my printing teacher knew I was good, so he wanted me to go to college for printing. So when I graduated, I didn't want to be me. I joined the Marine Corps like my big brother. I was mommy's boy, so I got out of it. I had a friend named Danny who stayed in, but he got hurt and was also discharged.

By this time, I wanted to be like my dad, so I started to work in a body shop. I never stayed in one place long. I moved from New Jersey to Oregon to California to Michigan. I took my drinking everywhere and didn't care about anybody. I didn't care who I hurt. When I was twenty-two, I was homeless and ran into a Marine Corps Recruiter. It had been five years since I went in the Marine Corps, so I joined back up. I was older now and was working out with the Marine Corps recruiter and I was ready now. At boot camp in California, I was at the rifle range when my knee and ankle gave out. I was discharge again. The first time I didn't want to be there; the second time my body didn't want to be there. I trained for it, and I was broken because I wanted to finally be a Marine. I felt sick inside.

My commanding officer told me I couldn't get anything from the Marine Corps. I didn't know about the Disabled American Veterans, so I took him at his word. Still drinking to forget that my life was a mess, I ran into a person named Tommy, who owned River Drive Collision. So, I went back to New Jersey and started to work for him. I was living in a rooming house and thought that if I was married maybe my life would be different.

The lady that ran and owned the rooming house wanted me to meet an Italian girl named Josephine. At that time I began dating Josephine, but at the same time I was dating a black girl and a Columbian girl. I didn't know what I wanted. I ended up marrying the Italian girl. We had this Barbie doll wedding with limos and a white Rolls-Royce. More than a hundred

and twenty people were there. It was just a big party. I was twenty-six years old.

My new wife wanted to change me, but it didn't work. She wanted to run the house and try to stop me from drinking, but that didn't work either. My oldest brother was my best man. Everybody was making bets on how long the marriage would last. We moved six blocks from her family. My brother laughed and teased that I was supposed to bring her to my farm, not move to hers.

Our marriage was a mess—we didn't get along and were angry at each other all the time. Every time I paid the rent she would put me out. One time she put me out with the police, and one night I got my first DWI. I left her because there was too much damage done. She started dating a married man that she had met on the job. I tried to go back to the Columbian girl, but she didn't want me.

I was drinking every night by now. I got a good job at a body shop in Fairlawn and met a woman named Diane. She worked at a luncheon in Farlawn, and I worked two blocks away. I would go there for coffee in the morning, and we would talk before I left for work. But I had just gotten a divorce from Josephine, and the last thing I wanted to do was get involved with somebody. I started dating Diane, and she would bring me dinner on Tuesdays and Thursdays because I worked late those nights. She sent a belly dancer to me on my thirtieth birthday. I fell in love. Of the same year I devorce Josephine

I had known Dianne for only three months, we married which was stupid, and we had a child in that year also, on August 30, 1988; we named her Kristina. I was a dad, and I told myself I would never be like the father I had, but I started drinking for any reason. My daughter would need food, and I would go to the bar. I was drinking more than anything. I didn't know if I could be a good father.

The acorn doesn't fall far from the tree—I was turning into my father. Diane would put me out, take me back, and continue this pattern for a while. I met a person from A.A. who told me I had to change my way of thinking. Diane didn't want me to get sober, because she would lose control. When I worked to stay sober, she would make me angry, and I would start drinking again. I would pay the rent, and she would put me out. I was reliving my first marriage, but I couldn't leave my daughter.

We lost apartments ?? because of my drinking or our fighting. We moved to Sussex for a weekend she left me with her ex-husband and ex-boyfriend they were all friends. Diane had a daughter by her ex-husband, and he didn't want to let go. She was supposed to marry her ex-boyfriend; it never happened, but they remained friends. I was brought into this sick situation. I lost all of my furniture, so I had to start all over. I was still drinking, and he wanted to raise my daughter. I thought she should have a daddy, but I still wasn't changing. We got an apartment in Elmwood Park, New Jersey, a block away from

her ex-husband. We lost that apartment too, and then we got our last apartment Garfield. I was working in a body shop in ?? and was trying to keep the marriage together. But I lost my job, and when I didn't have any money, she put me out. It was then that I knew I had married Satan's daughter—she turned so bad.

When my daughter was born, Diane was set in her ways. Her daughter was about sixteen or seventeen years old, and Kristina's birth put a stop to her single life. I paid for it. I was working at another body shop. I always made good money, but Diane wanted more and more money all the time. She thought she was raising a holy child from Jesus Himself. She took me to court for extra money and ended up with less. I noticed she had smoke coming out of her head she was so angry. She told me I would never see my daughter again. My daughter became a loaded gun to me; she pushed all my buttons.

I started to drink heavier. I got hurt on the job. she ?? Because of the injury I sustained in the Marine Corps, my ?? was weak. I had pain, but I learned to deal with it. My wife lived up to her word, and I wasn't seeing my daughter. I had a job at this body shop, and my leg was injured, so I couldn't work. I use to drink in a Puerto Rican bar, and they had a sister that worked for a lawyer. He handled my case. I was injured in 1993, but I didn't have the surgery I needed until 1994. However, it didn't work. I was drinking heavily and bouncing in and out of A.A. It wasn't working, and I just wanted to die.

I was celebrating surgeries like birthdays, one every year. In 1997, I was totally disabled, and in 2000, I had a complete knee replacement. I still wasn't seeing my daughter in these years. I was bouncing in and out of detox programs. Still drinking, I ended up in a hotel called Winslow. It was April 24, 2000. The next day I called A.A., and they tried to take me to another detox, but I didn't want it. They took my to the liquor store and bought me beer and a bottle of vodka and let me drink so I couldn't fight with them anymore.

Later, they took me to the hospital. I was so drunk they put me in a wheelchair to get me into the hospital. I woke up in a detox and didn't know where I was. I was a blackout drinker, so I was use to it. My niece's birthday is April 25, and that was the day I stopped drinking. Every year she celebrates a birthday, and I celebrate another year sober. When I walked out of that detox, I asked Jesus to take the drinking. I knew how to get drunk, but I had to remain teachable on how to get sober. My life was a mess, so I took all the advice from A.A. and my sponsor. I drank for thirty years, so it was hard. I couldn't figure out how somebody could not drink on holidays, birthdays, Christmas, New Year's, my mom's birthday, my sister's, the dog's birthday, the cat's birthday. I used any excuse to drink, any reason I could think of—I was sick. I knew then that I was my dad's son. Now any day with a great drunk doesn't make up for any bad day sober.

I had to live my life in a different way. One day when I had been sober for eight months I had to meet my mom for breakfast. I had a bad cold, and my eyes were bloodshot. The first thing out of my mom's mouth was to ask if I had been drinking. When you try to get sober for twelve years, people don't trust you. I was angry about it, but my sponsor explained that I had screwed people around, so why should they trust me. Just because you stop doesn't mean they stop thinking.

After a year and a half, I met another girl. I had just gotten a car and saw her catching a bus with her girlfriend. I picked them up at a bus stop one day when it was cold. Her name was Maria, and she was Columbian. It was funny—she couldn't speak English, and I couldn't speak Spanish, but we fell in love.

I continue with A.A., and my life has changed. The VA finally took care of the responsibility after screwing me out of 20 years of benefits before,they gave me nothing. What happen to all the money they screwed me out of? I moved to North Carolina in 2003, and in 2005 I bought my first home. In 2006 I was found to be 100 percent disabled by the VA. My legs are really bad now, but that's no reason to drink. I finally met my daughter when she was seventeen years old. The last time I had seen her she was four years old. When we reconnected, she was a mess. Her mother had her in and out of foster care and put her on medication to collect Social Security. I tried to work with her, and I couldn't.

My sister and my niece Rob my mother for second time. Her daughter was half black, so I was angry because her father was a piece of garbage too. My sister had something to do with this. Christmas Eve of 2006 my niece Latonia died at the age of thirty-three. My sister and her screwed my mother, so the rest of the family turned against my sister but I tried to help her. But she had no ??, and I had to stop. I even gave her one of my cars to use.

My brother is still drinking. I tried to help him, but he's another person who could take advantage of somebody. He stayed with me for five months. He stayed sober, but he was crazy as hell. I guess he wanted to drink more than he wanted to get sober. He hit me in the head with a pipe, so I put him out.

My little sister takes care of my mother now. She's a little like my dad—she doesn't take anything from anybody. She has two kids who are also half black, but they're really good kids.

Now me: I married that girl I met at the bus stop. Life isn't the greatest, but I have my life back today. I keep my memory green. I did some bad things drinking.

I did some things I'm not proud of. I never stopped loving my mother. You know, all the years I drank I never took a dime from my mother. I'm going on ten years sober now and look at my life—it was a living hell. I was molested by friends and my father, the man who I respected and loved the most. God knows that if I can do it, you can too. Give A.A. a chance. Change, find your faith in Jesus, talk to people, find meetings, and keep your memory green. Life is better sober. People won't believe in the beginning, but after awhile, they'll see the change. Save two dollars a day for ninety days. After that, you'll have a $180. If your life hasn't gotten any better than before you stopped, go and refund all your money back. Books and pills won't get you sober—only A.A. will.

I hope my story has helped somebody out. Life isn't easy, but you can deal with it better by being sober. If nobody told you that they love you, I do. God bless you!

Alcoholism is something that can attack anybody. It doesn't matter who you are—whether you live on Park Avenue or Park Bench. I've met people that lost everything living in the streets, begging for money. I went to every detox in the state of New Jersey. I was introduced to A.A. seriously in 1987. It took me thirteen years to get sober, because I wanted to do it my way. I'm not Frank Sinatra—I had to do it A.A.'s way.

I was living in a rooming house with no car when I became sober. I was disabled. Now I own a house, and I have four cars. Life has changed. Learn to love yourself before you can love somebody else. I even forgive everybody for hurting me, including my father. You can't remain sober until you learn to forgive.

One last thing: there are books on how you can get sober and pills you can take. Believe me, if people read these books and take pills, there wouldn't be A.A. The books and pills are bullshit. Just get involved with A.A. and join the winners. I know my childhood and being hurt in the military had a lot to do with my drinking.

The military didn't want to take responsibility for what it did to me until the year 2000, twenty years after the accident happened. They talk about today's military, but they forget about yesterday's military; there are a lot of women dealing with the same problems from the military that I have.

My only dream is that I could help kids with the same hell I went through and try to change them around. Children only learn what their parents teach them. Then they learn the rest on the streets. You have to show kids love and attention. If they're treated badly and hurt the way I was, they turn to alcohol and drugs to get rid of the hurt or to be something they're not. Drinking made me into a dancer, a fighter, and a lover. Now I'm sober, and I'm me.

You know, I couldn't figure out why my father sent me to work when I was only ten years old. All my friends were playing baseball and having fun, and I was working. I think I was reliving his life.

The other things that happen to me as a child were also extremely painful. I learned a lot about my family as I got older. My grandparents were related, and Italian people also have a lot of pride. My mother told my father that he looked like a Puerto Rican who should go on welfare. My dad said that he was not a beggar. I remember every Saturday all the parents would sit outside and drink beer and talk, and when they weren't looking, I would steal some beer.

I've learned a lot since I became sober. I was crying for help, and nobody was listening. My sisters and brother cared about themselves. It's hard. At times, my older sister is a con artist, and my little sister doesn't show her elders any respect. One thing I can say is that she loves our mother like I do.

My older sister ?? robbed my mother with her daughter. Her daughter died two days before her thirty-fourth birthday. Every year on Christmas Eve my sister still suffers over her death. I guess it is a constant reminder.

My older brother doesn't care about anybody. He's still drinking and getting DWIs everywhere he goes. He only cries when he needs help. I took him in two or three times, and he hit me in the head with a pipe after I paid money to help him to be able to drive again. He left after I helped him and went to Michigan and lost his driver's license for drunk driving. He screwed me again, but he keeps sober by his mistakes.

I guess every family has problems. My family just had a little more than others, I guess. That's why I made as many mistakes as I did. The best thing that happened to me was wife Maria. I did a lot of things to better myself, like buying a house. I didn't think I would turn my life around like that, and it only took a good woman. My other wives couldn't clean her doorstep.

Drinking was easy for me. I was drinking for thirty years. I had to remain teachable to become sober. My sponsor told me I should let everything out, and that would begin the healing. I also had to make amends with everybody I hurt, and I had to forgive everybody who hurt me. That was hard. I had to forgive my father—he hurt me the most, but, God will tell you that if I don't forgive him, God don't forgive me. Every bad day sober is better than every good day drunk. I thank A.A. for saving my life.

I remember when I first became sober, people would pick me up and take me to meetings. I had a habit of driving people crazy, but the only ass I can save is my own!

You can lead a horse to water, but you can't make him drink it.

You don't have to get sober unless you admit you're powerless over alcohol. Your mom, dad, wife, brother, sister, dog, cat, bird—they're all excuses. You have to do it for yourself. A pill or book won't get you sober only A.A. I tried. It's one alcoholic working with another alcoholic . I just want to tell you a story. I recieved a D.W.I. in New Jersey and I had to hire a lawyer. This lawyer told me he represented a man who had millions; he got drunk and hit a sixteen year old girl on a bike and killed her; all the money he had didn't stop him from going to prison for twenty years. This could happen to you if you have a drinking problem. I hope my story has helped somebody, and if nobody told you they love you, I do. God Bless You and may God be with you........ *William Tedesco*